LEGACY KITCHEN
1219

"An Inheritance of Recipes from

My Family to Yours"

Javon McCain-Nicholas

Dedicated to my Grandparents

Mr. Robert R. Davis and Mrs. Gertrude M. Davis

My Mother

Judith E. Davis McCain-Brown

My Beloved

Aunties, Uncles, Cousins, Father and Family Friends

PREFACE

My Grandmother prepared the most creative and taste tantalizing meals out of a tiny kitchen like the one posted above. I never heard her complain about the task of preparing such large meals or the size of the kitchen she had to do it in. We as a family knew that we had two people who loved us, provided for us and nourished our bodies with wisdom and comforting meals that would turn into pathways of delicious memories. Thank you, family, for all of the joyous times we shared at **1219**. I dedicate this culinary memoir to my grandparents who fell in love and built a life surrounded by family and friends. You fed our bodies, hearts and souls and I am forever grateful and proud to be a part of your

Legacy.

Love,

Javon McCain-Nicholas

TABLE OF CONTENTS

THE PATRIARCH - KING OF THE FAMILY

Robert Richmond Davis was born the eldest of eight children and was forced to drop out of sixth grade to help his parents and siblings live a better and stable life. He was in the "C. C. Camp, U.S Army and a Pullman Porter. Because of his generous heart, hard work and dedication my family was able to have a beautiful life on the South side of Chicago in a community named Marynook.

My Grandfather was a "Manly Man" who built things with his bare hands like the brick layered BBQ pit pictured above. Each year my grandparents would host a Lua and my Granddaddy would tend to the apple mouth stuffed hog until golden brown and crisp for the entire neighborhood to enjoy.

He was a loving and spiritual man that sung "Life is like a mountains railroad "in a quartet growing up. He taught us the true meaning of family and family values. He taught us about hard work and great work ethic. Lastly, he taught us this toast that is sweet and "Best" just like him!

"Luck to the duck that swam up the stream

And never lost a feather

I pray this time next year

We'll all still be together"!

THE MATRIARCH - QUEEN OF THE KITCHEN

Gertrude Davis affectionately called "Nanny" was the strongest woman I have ever known. She could do anything that she put her mind too especially when it came down to cooking. She was my favorite "Red Haired lady" 'A Fox" as some would call her. She loved hard and cursed people out even harder but hey that was her way sometimes. She was a strong Capricorn as she would warn others when they would challenge her intelligence or view point.

My Nanny was a nurturer not only to babies but to people in need. I've heard stories about her helping people off of heroin in the 1950's, monitoring babies with SID's, adopting abandoned children that were left behind in the Foster Care system and raising them as her own and more!

Besides being in the nursing field, my Nanny was a seamstress, hairdresser, and caterer to say the least. I could watch her for hours as she would cook our daily scratched made meals in the tiniest of tiny kitchens. We would feast on homemade traditional soul food and a diverse spread of goodies like tacos, beef chop suey, jerk chicken, and ham fried rice. I would sit at the table and watch her every move. She would sometimes give me miniature pans to create a tiny version of a cake she was baking.

She knew how to make a person feel protected, loved, beautiful and spoiled completely rotten! Whose Grandmother would hire a limousine service to surprise their grandkids with an all expense paid Amtrak trip to Walt Disney World eight years in a row? My Nanny did!

THE CHILDREN - THE LEGACY

These beautifully talented five are the children of Robert and Gertrude Davis. My Aunts, Uncles and Mother. My Auntie Ruby loved fried chicken wings, dancing, singing, being the life of the party. She was an amazing seamstress and collected dress shoes and videotapes. My Uncle Adolph (Charles) was a "ladies' man", very intelligent and brawny. He was very independent and an amazing cook as well who loved "Hoppin John" and neckbones with rice.

My Uncle Shug (Robert) was amazingly handsome, intelligent and protective. He was extremely close to his younger sisters and would participate in their make-believe roles such as "The Three Musketeers, The Three Stooges and the Mickey Mouse Club. Although his life was short lived, my Mother made sure that I knew about his loving spirit, vitality and creativeness. When I was born, he wrote a song for me and named it "Ashia's Theme".

My Mother was Judith who adored her baby sister Kathryn. My Auntie Kathryn "Chatty Kathy" was a living doll as a young girl. She loved to be spoiled and dressed in beautiful dresses with gloves and ruffle socks. Till this day she adores being "The Baby" and lives to carry on the love, life and legacy of her parents and siblings.

RECIPES FOR BREAKFAST, BRUNCH AND THE BOUGIE

Nanny's Salmon Croquettes

NANNY'S SAUSAGE AND SMOTHERED POTATO SKILLET

Prep time: 15 mins

Cook time: 30 mins

Total time: 45 mins

Serves: 6

Quick and easy!

Ingredients

- 4 pounds of Idaho potatoes peeled and sliced
- 2 large sweet onions, sliced
- 1 large bell pepper, diced (optional)
- 1 pack of smoked kielbasa or andouille sausage, sliced
- 2 teaspoons of minced garlic
- 1 tsp of Cajun seasoning to taste
- 1 tsp of ground black pepper
- 1 TBSP of granulated onion powder
- 1 TBSP of granulated garlic powder
- 1 tsp of seasoning salt to taste
- 1 tsp of paprika
- ¼ cup of cooking oil
- ½ cup of water

Directions

1. Cut potatoes in ¼" slices.
2. In a bowl mix dry potato with seasonings and set aside.
3. In a skillet with oil pan fry sliced sausages until crisp on all sides.

4. Take sausage out of pan and set aside.

5. De glaze the skillet by pouring water into the skillet and stir the meat drippings.

6. Add seasoned potatoes and sausages to the skillet.

7. Put on medium heat and stir together until mixture begins to steam.

8. Cover pot, turn heat to low, and stir frequently until potatoes are tender.

NANNY'S BRUNCH LEFTOVER ROAST BEEF HASH

Prep time: 15 mins

Cook time: 30 mins

Total time: 45 mins

Serves: 6

Quick and easy!

Ingredients

- 2 cups leftover roast beef, sliced into small cubes
- 1 large sweet onion, diced small
- 1 large bell pepper, diced small
- 4 pounds of Idaho potatoes, diced small
- 2 teaspoons of minced garlic
- 1 TBSP of ground black pepper
- 1 TBSP of granulated onion powder
- 1 TBSP of granulated garlic powder
- 1 tsp of seasoning salt to taste
- 4 TBSP of flour
- ¼ cup of cooking oil
- 2 tsp oil to sauté meat and potatoes
- ½ cup of water

Directions

1. In a bow mix dry potatoes with salt, black pepper, minced garlic, garlic and onion powder and set aside.
2. In a large pot add 1 tsp of oil, roast beef and seasoned potatoes.

3. Mix together until lightly brown, remove and set aside.

4. Mix flour and oil in the pot and stir continuously to create a roux for gravy.

5. Stir until creamy like "Peanut butter."

6. Add water and stir.

7. Add seasoned potatoes and beef to the pot.

8. Put on medium heat and stir together until mixture begins to steam.

9. Cover pot, turn heat to low, and stir frequently until potatoes are tender.

10. Serve on top of white rice with a side of biscuits for a filling dish!

COUSIN'S ALEX'S STRAWBERRY SWIRL OATMEAL

Prep time: 10 mins

Cook time: 10 mins

Total time: 20 mins

Serves: 4

Quick and easy!

Ingredients

- 4 cups of choice of oats
- pinch of kosher salt
- 4 cups of milk (of any kind)
- 4 cups of water
- 2 cups hulled and roughly chopped fresh strawberries, plus additional 1/2 cup diced strawberries
- 3 TBSP of raw honey
- 1 tsp vanilla extract

Directions

1. Place oats, milk, water and salt in a medium sauce pot.
2. Cook oats, stirring frequently over medium heat until thickened, about 10-15 minutes.
3. Blend 2 cups of chopped strawberries with honey in a blender and blend until smooth and creamy.
4. Pour strawberry mixture into a small sauce pan and stir in vanilla extract.
5. Cook low and slow until thick stirring constantly.
6. Once oatmeal has thickened place in individual bowls or large casserole dish.
7. Create a large swirl pattern on top of the cooked oatmeal with a heightened spoon and enjoy!

NANNY'S SALMON CROQUETTES

Prep time: 10 mins

Cook time: 10 mins

Total time: 20 mins

Serves: 10

Quick and easy!

Ingredients

- 2 cans of pink salmon
- 1 large sweet onion, diced
- 1 large bell pepper, diced
- 2 tsp of finely minced green onion
- 2 eggs, beaten
- 2 teaspoons of minced garlic
- 1 tsp of Cajun seasoning to taste
- 1 tsp of ground black pepper
- 1 TBSP of granulated onion powder
- 1 TBSP of granulated garlic powder
- 1 tsp of seasoning salt to taste
- 1 tsp of paprika
- ¼ cup of cooking oil
- ½ cup of yellow cornmeal
- ½ cup of all-purpose flour
- 3 tbsp of all-purpose flour for thickening
- 1 TBSP of baking powder (secret ingredient)
- Oil for pan frying

Directions

1. Drain and discard salmon juice from the can.
2. In a bowl use a fork to break down the meat of the salmon and discard bones if desired.
3. Add onions, bell peppers, seasonings and mix thoroughly.
4. Add beaten eggs and mix.
5. Add 3 tbsp of all-purpose flour and mix.
6. In a Ziploc bag or shallow pan mix all purpose flour, baking powder and cornmeal together.
7. Hand form salmon into 10 patties and flatten.
8. Coat in flour mixture and fry immediately in a skillet with heated oil.
9. Cook on both sides until crust is golden and crispy.
10. Enjoy with rice, grits, scrambled eggs and biscuits!

NANNY'S "SOMETHING SPECIAL" CHICKEN SALAD

Prep time: 15 mins

Cook time: 25 mins

Total time: 35 mins

Serves: 8

Delicious!

Ingredients

- 3 pounds of boneless skinless chicken breast or 2 ¼ pounds of leftover cooked chicken (Omit broth/stock)
- 4 cups of chicken or vegetable broth/stock
- 1 ¼ cup of mayonnaise plus more to desired taste
- 4 cups of shredded broccoli slaw mix
- 1 large purple onion, finely minced
- 6 sprigs of fresh green onion, finely minced
- ½ cup of sweet pickled relish
- 2 teaspoons of minced garlic
- 1 tsp of ground black pepper
- 1 TBSP of granulated onion powder
- 1 TBSP of granulated garlic powder
- 1 tsp of seasoning salt to taste
- 1 tsp of paprika for garnish
- 1 tsp of dried parsley for garnish
- 1 TBSP of dried parsley
- 1 tsp of hot sauce (Secret ingredient)

Directions

1. Boil chicken in broth/stock until fully cooked, set aside and refrigerate.
2. In a large bowl make a "slurry" using the mayonnaise, hot sauce and all seasonings except for the garnishes.
3. Taste for desired balance of flavor.
4. Once chicken is cooked and manageable, shred the chicken into small pieces using a fork.
5. Add shredded chicken, chopped onions and broccoli slaw to slurry and mix thoroughly.
6. Add more mayo if the salad seems dry however, the salad will absorb the "Slurry" overnight so please be careful with the mayo.
7. Garnish with paprika and dried parsley, serve chilled with Bougie crackers and enjoy!

Sherbet Punch (Frappe')

OLD SCHOOL COTILLION FINGER SANDWICHES AND SHERBET PUNCH (FRAPPE)
TUNA, CRAB, CUCUMBER

Prep time: 15 mins

Cook time: 0 mins

Total time: 15 mins

Serves: 6

Fillings

- 2 loaves of white bread or 36 large slices (crust removed) 1 pound of prepared tuna salad, crab salad, or 2 thinly sliced English cucumbers
- 1/2 cup of cream cheese
- 2 TBSP of miracle whip or mayonnaise with sugar to taste
- 1 Tsp of dried parsley
- 1 Tsp of dried dill for cucumber sandwiches
- Freshly cracked black pepper as desired
- Paprika as desired for garnish

Directions

1. Cut crustless bread into triangles or rectangles then lay out 3 rows of 12 slices of bread.
2. If coloring bread: Mix desired food coloring in water and set aside.
3. Use a pastry brush and lightly color all sides of the bread and set aside to dry.
4. Mix the cream cheese and miracle whip together in a bowl thoroughly.
5. Spread a thin layer of cream cheese mayo mixture on both sides of bread.

6. Layer tuna salad, crab salad or cucumbers on top of cream cheese mayo mixture.

7. Garnish with black pepper, dried parsley, paprika and dill if desired.

8. Top sandwiches and serve on a platter and be Bougie!

SHERBET PUNCH (FRAPPE')

Prep time: 5 mins

Cook time: 0 mins

Total time: 5 mins

Serves: 20

Ingredients

- 1 gallon of Raspberry or desired Sherbet
- 16 cups of Cranberry Juice or Fruit punch 100% juice, well chilled
- 2 2- liters bottles of Ginger Ale, well chilled

Directions

1. Scoop out Sherbet into a decanter or Bougie bowl, add juice and top with ginger ale. Stir, garnish with fresh berries and serve immediately Enjoy!

NOSTALGIC RECIPES

Cousin Kyra, Auntie Kathy and Javon

We rarely ate fast food growing up. Besides an occasional" Happy Meal" from our neighborhood McDonald's restaurant, My Auntie, Uncle and cousin would save me some of their KFC dinner from their annual road trips to 1219. I would wait up as long as I was allowed, hug them and get my plate of original fried chicken, mashed potato and biscuit. Now sure it was leftover and cold but it was the best ever coming from them!

Sometimes my Nanny would treat us to a Chicago style deep dish pizza. We would go to Gino's East at their original location downtown on Superior and sit in "the dark dungeon" as I called it which was the lower level of the restaurant. We would wait for what seemed for hours to get our mega slices of pizza in which my uncle Robert would refer to as a "quiche" and I couldn't devour more than two slices in one sitting. Nostalgic memories indeed and I hope you enjoy my recipe!

Chicago style deep dish pizza

CHICAGO STYLE DEEP DISH PIZZA

Total time: 7 hrs 25 mins includes dough rising time

Serves: 8 slices 10 to 12 in deep dish pan

Ingredients

- 1 lb. Italian sausage, mild and bulk
- 1 28-ounce can San Marzano tomatoes, crushed
- 1 packet of Active dry yeast
- ½ cup of warm water (110 to 115 F)
- ¼ cups of All-purpose flour
- 1/8 tsp of cream of tartar
- 1 tsp granulated sugar to add to yeast
- 1 Tbsp of Granulated sugar
- 2 tsp of fine sea salt
- 1 Tbsp of dried oregano
- 1 Tbsp of dried basil
- 8 to 12 slices of part skim mozzarella cheese
- 1/3 cup of finely grated parmesan
- 2 ¼ tsp of corn oil
- 1 Tbsp of annatto food coloring (It's the secret ingredient for the" Cornmeal color")

Directions

1. Mix sugar, yeast and room temperature water in a bowl and let bloom for 15 minutes. Once yeast has bloomed add to combined flour, salt and cream of tartar in the bowl of a stand mixer OR mix by hand in a bowl for 10 minutes.

2. Lightly coat a large bowl with corn oil and cover bowl with a towel and let rest for 3 hours or until double in size. In a deep-dish pan lightly coat pan and place ball of dough in the center of pan. Using butter coated hands, gently push dough in an outward motion until the crust is formed and completely covered the pan. Gently tug the dough upwards to form the crust edges and make sure the dough is as even as possible all the way around.

3. Position an oven rack in the middle of the oven and preheat to 450 ° degrees F.

4. Cover entire bottom in mozzarella, all the way up to the edge. Cover with an even layer of raw sausage.

5. Mix in a bowl tomatoes, sugar, salt, oregano and basil. Top raw sausage with a couple handfuls of crushed tomatoes mixture.

6. Spread out with hands to the edge. Sprinkle top evenly with grated Parmesan.

   Bake, rotating halfway through, until golden around the edge, about 25 minutes. The pizza might take an hour depending on the oven. Let rest for about 5 minutes on a wire rack in the pan and gently lift pizza out of pan and enjoy!

Cousin Shirley's Hawaiian fruit salad

COUSIN SHIRLEY'S HAWAIIAN FRUIT SALAD

Prep time: 10 mins

Cook time: n/a

Total time: 4 hrs. 10 mins mins

Serves: 10

Delicious!

Ingredients

- 1 can of crushed pineapple, drained thoroughly
- 1 can of pineapple chunks, drained thoroughly
- ¾ cup of shredded sweetened coconut
- 1- 8 ounce can of mandarin oranges, drained thoroughly
- 1 bag of miniature marshmallows
- 2 cups of cool whip cream
- 2 cups of sour cream
- 1- packet of vanilla flavored pudding, dry
- ½ cup of chopped walnuts
- 1 jar of maraschino cherries, drained thoroughly

Directions

1. Freeze the mixing bowl for 20 minutes before mixing salad together.
2. Add1 tablespoon of pineapple juice from the can to cool whip.
3. Mix in sour cream and vanilla pudding and stir.
4. Add all pineapple and mandarin oranges to mixture.
5. Mix in the bag of marshmallows and coconut.
6. Add walnuts and cherries last and mix.
7. Cover and put in the fridge until ready to serve.

NANNY'S PAN-FRIED COLLARD GREENS WITH BACON AND GRANDDADDY'S HOT WATER CORNBREAD

Prep time: 15 mins

Cook time: 30 mins

Total time: 45 mins

Serves: 4

A perfect side dish

Ingredients

- 2 pounds of fresh collard greens washed and chopped small
- 6 Rind on thick slices of preferred bacon, chopped
- If using turkey or chicken bacon use 9 slices and add 1/3 cup of chicken stock or 1 tbsp of bouillon for extra flavor
- 2 cloves of garlic, crushed
- If using turkey or chicken bacon use 1/3 cup of shortening which is preferred or a neutral oil JUST NO Olive Oil (The taste will drastically change)
- 1 to 2 tbsp of seasoning salt to taste
- 1 tsp of granulated onion powder
- 1 tsp of granulated garlic powder
- 1 tsp of dried red chili flakes
- 1 tsp of white sugar to balance flavors
- 1 tsp of baking soda (secret for tenderizing the collard greens in such a short period of time)"

Directions

1. Add chopped bacon to a large cast iron preferred skillet over medium heat. Cook bacon, stirring occasionally, until crispy, about 5 minutes. Use a slotted spoon to remove from the pan and set aside, leaving the fat in the pan. (See tip if not using pork bacon).
2. Add the garlic to the bacon grease and cook until fragrant.
3. Add the greens, baking soda, seasonings, and stir.
4. Cook the greens, covered with a lid stirring occasionally, until greens are nice and tender.

Granddaddy's hot water cornbread

Ingredients:

1 1/2 cup of cornmeal

1 tsp of baking soda

1 tsp of white sugar

2 tbsp of butter

½ cup of flour

¼ tsp salt

¾ cup of boiling water

In a medium bowl, combine cornmeal, flour, baking soda, salt and sugar mix thoroughly. Lastly add butter and then stir in boiling water mixing constantly until stir until butter melts. Form cornmeal mixture into patties. In a large skillet with an 1/2 inch of oil in depth, heat to 375 degrees F and fry until golden on both sides. Serve immediately with Nanny's Greens and Enjoy!

NANNY'S HOMESTYLE MASHED POTATOES

Prep time: 15 mins

Cook time: 15 mins

Total time: 30 mins

Serves: 6

Delicious!

Ingredients

- 4 pounds of Idaho potatoes, peeled and diced small
- 2 teaspoons of minced garlic
- 1 TBSP of ground white pepper
- 1 TBSP of granulated onion powder
- 1 TBSP of granulated garlic powder
- 1 tsp of seasoning salt to taste
- 2 TBSP of dried parsley
- 4 TBSP of unsalted butter
- 1 can of evaporated milk

Directions

1. In a stockpot filled halfway with cold water, add cleaned peeled potatoes.
2. Once potatoes are fork tender drain water using a colander.
3. Return potatoes to stockpot and add white pepper and salt to taste, onion powder, garlic powder, parsley, minced garlic, butter and milk.
4. Mash until fluffy and creamy. Return to stove on low heat, constantly stirring and until bubbling hot. Top with more butter and serve.

NANNY'S PARSLIED POTATOES

Prep time: 15 mins

Cook time: 15 mins

Total time: 30 mins

Serves: 6

Delicious!

Ingredients

- 4 pounds of red potatoes, peeled and whole in size
- 2 teaspoons of minced garlic
- 1 TBSP of ground white pepper
- 1 TBSP of granulated onion powder
- 1 TBSP of granulated garlic powder
- 1 tsp of seasoning salt to taste
- 3 TBSP of dried parsley
- 2 Tsp of fresh parsley minced finely
- 4 TBSP of unsalted butter

Directions

1. In a stockpot filled halfway with cold water, add cleaned peeled potatoes, and dried parsley and boil.
2. Once potatoes are fork tender drain water using a colander.
3. Return potatoes to stockpot and add white pepper and salt to taste, onion powder, garlic powder, parsley, minced garlic and butter.
4. Mix up and return to stove on low heat, quickly stirring until butter is melted and serve.

NANNY'S FRESH CUCUMBER SALAD

Prep time: 15 mins

Cook time: 15 mins

Total time: 30 mins

Serves: 6

Delicious!

Ingredients

- 4 pounds of red potatoes, peeled and whole in size
- 2 teaspoons of minced garlic
- 1 TBSP of ground white pepper
- 1 TBSP of granulated onion powder
- 1 TBSP of granulated garlic powder
- 1 tsp of seasoning salt to taste
- 3 TBSP of dried parsley
- 2 Tsp of fresh parsley minced finely
- 4 TBSP of unsalted butter

Directions

1. In a stockpot filled halfway with cold water, add cleaned peeled potatoes, and dried parsley and boil.
2. Once potatoes are fork tender drain water using a colander.
3. Return potatoes to stockpot and add white pepper and salt to taste, onion powder, garlic powder, parsley, minced garlic and butter.
4. Mix up and return to stove on low heat, quickly stirring until butter is melted and serve.

NANNY'S SAUTEED SPINACH WITH CHOPPED EGG GARNISH

Prep time: 10 mins

Cook time: 10 mins

Total time: 20 mins

Serves: 5

Delicious and keto friendly!

Ingredients

- 4 pounds of fresh spinach, clean and leafy
- 2 teaspoons of minced garlic
- 1 TBSP of ground white pepper
- 1 TBSP of granulated onion powder
- 1 TBSP of granulated garlic powder
- 1 tsp of seasoning salt to taste
- 3 hard boiled eggs, cooled and diced into cubes
- 4 TBSP of unsalted butter

Directions

1. In a saucepan add butter and minced garlic and sauté until fragrant.
2. Add spinach, and seasonings and stir.
3. If pan is dry add 1 to tsp of water but be careful not to add too much!
4. Once the spinach and ingredients are incorporated, serve in a bowl garnished with chopped boiled eggs and Enjoy!

AUNT KATHY'S LEFTOVER TURKEY TURKEY POT PIE

Prep time: 15 mins

Cook time: 20 mins

Total time: 35 mins

Serves: 6

Ingredients

- 2 Pre made pie crust
- 2 Pie crust lids
- 1 lb.: Cooked leftover turkey or cooked chicken
- 2 cans of condensed cream of chicken soup
- 12 ounces of frozen peas and carrots
- 1 cup of diced fresh potatoes
- 1 TBSP of ground white pepper
- 1 TBSP of granulated onion powder
- 1 TBSP of granulated garlic powder
- 1 tsp of seasoning salt to taste
- 3 TBSP of dried parsley
- 1/8 Tsp of poultry seasoning
- 1 cup of water (for the potatoes and veggies)

Directions

1. In a stockpot fill with cold water, add cleaned peeled diced potatoes and veggies cook for 8 to 10 minutes.
2. Once potatoes are fork tender drain water using a colander.

3. In a bowl mix turkey, cooked potatoes, veggies, condensed cream of chicken soup and seasoning until well incorporated.

4. Once mixed pour mixture into pie shells.

5. Spread mixture evenly and top with pie lid.

6. Press and secure pie lid using a fork.

7. Pierce 4 holes using a fork on top of pie lids to release pressure while cooking. Bake in oven at 375° F until golden brown.

Aunt Kathy's Italian cream cake

AUNT KATHY'S ITALIAN CREAM CAKE

Prep time: 15 mins

Cook time: 45 mins

Total time: 60 mins

Serves: 6

Delicious!

Ingredients

- 1 stick of Butter
- ½ cup of vegetable oil
- 2 cups of sugar
- 5 Egg separated (beat egg whites stiffly)
- 1 cup of buttermilk
- 1 Tsp. Baking soda
- 2 cups of cake flour
- 1 Tsp of pure vanilla extract
- 1 cup of sweetened shredded coconut
- ½ cup chopped pecans

Frosting

- 1-8 oz Cream cheese, softened
- 1 stick of Butter, softened
- 1 pound of powdered sugar
- 1 Tsp pure vanilla extract
- Chopped pecans for garnish

Directions

1. Cream butter, oil and sugar, add egg yolks one at a time, beating after each addition.
2. Stir baking soda into buttermilk. Add sifted flour into batter, alternating with buttermilk mixture. Add vanilla, coconut and chopped nuts.
3. Beat egg whites and flour into mixture. Pour into a greased and floured 9 x 13 – inch cake pan for a sheet cake, or three 8- or 9-inch layer pans. Bake at 325° degrees F for 45 minutes. Cool on cake rack.
4. Frosting: Beat cream cheese and butter, add vanilla, powder sugar and nuts, continue to beat until mixture reaches spreading consistency.
5. Frost cake, Top with extra pecans and enjoy!

GRANDDADDY'S FAVORITE FRIED GREEN TOMATO GRAVY

Prep time: 10 mins

Total time: 25 mins

Serves: 6

Courtesy of my Auntie Edna

Ingredients

- 8 Green tomatoes, sliced ½ "to ¾ "thick
- 2 cups of whole buttermilk
- 1 large egg, beaten
- 1 cups of yellow cornmeal
- ½ cup of all-purpose flour
- 1 cups of water reserve for gravy
- 1 cup of canned evaporated milk reserve for gravy
- 3 TBSP of seasoning salt
- 1 TBSP of granulated onion powder
- 1 TBSP of granulated garlic powder
- 1 tsp of black pepper
- Vegetable oil or shortening for deep frying

Directions

1. Select firm tomatoes using a serrated knife slice tomatoes into 1/4 – inch thick slices.
2. Soak tomato slices in buttermilk for at least 30 minutes.
3. Add seasonings to the cornmeal and set up dredging station with beaten egg in a bowl, and cornmeal in a bowl.

4. Use one hand for dry ingredients and the other for wet ingredients.

5. Dip one tomato slice at a time into egg bowl and then the cornmeal.

6. Arrange on a wire rack and use a large heavy, cast iron skillet heat oil on medium-high heat until the temperature reaches 350 F and fry each tomato until golden brown. Set tomatoes aside and turn off fire.

7. Reduce used oil in pan to ½ cup. Turn on fire and add flour once oil is heated. Stir with a wooden spoon until the color of peanut butter is reached. Add water and milk. Stir until well incorporated. Add cooked tomatoes to gravy and reduce heat until creamy good! Salt and pepper to taste and serve over rice, mashed potatoes, with fried chicken or biscuits! ENJOY!

Nanny's Strawberry cheesecake

NANNY'S HOMEMADE STRAWBERRY CHEESECAKE

Total time: 1 hr30 mins

Serves: 6

The Crust:

- 2 cups of Graham crackers, crushed
- ¼ cup of butter, unsalted and melted

The Filling and topping:

- ¼ lbs. of Cream cheese
- 4 Eggs, Large
- 1 tsp Lemon juice (reserve 1 tsp for glaze)
- 1 tsp lemon zest
- 1 cup of fresh strawberries
- 1 cup of strawberry preserve
- 2 TBSP of All-purpose flour
- 2 TBSP of brown sugar
- 3 TBSP of cornstarch
- 2 ½ cup of granulated sugar
- ½ tsp of salt
- 2 tsp of Vanilla extract, pure
- 1 cup of water
- 1/3 cup of sweet port dessert wine (optional)

Directions

1. Cheesecake Top: Wash and remove tops of strawberries. They will sit upside-down on the cheesecake.

2. Fresh Strawberry Glaze: Add to a small stockpot, 1 cup of sugar, strawberry preserve, lemon juice, water, port wine and cornstarch. Cook until topping comes to a boil stirring continuously with a wooden spoon. Set aside.

3. Preheat oven to 350° F.

4. Butter the sides and bottom of a 9-inch springform pan.

5. In a medium bowl, mix the graham cracker crumbs, melted butter and brown sugar until. completely combined/ Pour the mixture in the pan and press down firmly. Set aside.

6. In a small bowl, whisk together the granulated sugar, flour and salt. Set aside.

7. In a stand mixer bowl, beat the cream cheese on medium until smooth. Scrape down the sides. On medium low speed slowly add the flour/sugar mixture and beat until well incorporated. Scrape down the sides and speed up the mixture to medium.

8. Add the eggs one at a time, vanilla extract, lemon juice and lemon zest. Stop mixer and scrape down sides.

9. Mix until everything is creamy and smooth. Pour the cream cheese mixture into the pan over the crust and jiggle the mix to make sure everything is even.

10. Add ½ inch of water to an oversized baking pan and place cheesecake pan in the pan.

11. This will help the cheesecake cook evenly and not burn the crust!

12. Bake for 1 hour or until a knife comes out clean from the center of the cheesecake.

13. Let cool and pour half of the glaze on top of the cheesecake.

14. Add fresh strawberries, aligned and pointed in an upwards pattern.

15. Pour remaining glaze over the strawberries and refrigerate overnight or at least 2 hours.

16. Cut into beautiful slices and ENJOY!

THE COUSINS

These are the cousins that I was raised with at 1219 my family home. My cousin Shirley is my Grandmother's eldest niece and although she had her own home, we would see her consistently drop by the house, take us little cousins to Lincoln Park zoo, bring her famous Hawaiian salad to the annual BBQ's or Luau and she was our personal DJ as our family loved to dance!

My Cousin Eugene was raised as my Uncle and he had an amazing sense of humor, would take us bike riding and loved my Nanny's home cooking!

My cousin Faith was raised as my Aunt and I considered her as a second mom to me. Before she had children, I was with her night and day. She gave me an awesome middle name and till this day she is one of my biggest cheerleader's. Her tuna noodle casserole was created due to the limited amounts of ingredients she had in her cupboard. It is so delicious that it is the only way that I will eat tuna noodle casserole!

Scheree , Scharmaine, Mary and Gary along with Tiffany are my Uncle Shug's children and my cousins. I was raised with Tiffany spending the night, having slumber parties and gossiping on the phone with her friends. Tiffany loved my Nanny's collard greens and I used to watch her mix cornbread and collard greens together and feast.

Lastly my cousin Alex! Alex now is the eldest of five siblings but at 1219 she was an only child! She was more like a little sister than a cousin to me. The Tom Boy in her made our worlds kind of different considering that I had all Barbie dolls and she played with Ninja Turtles but at meal time we joined forces! I remember her going through this spell of time where she had to have strawberry oatmeal with a strawberry swirl. I called this my cousin Alex's strawberry swirl oatmeal and I hope that you all enjoy the recipe.

Some of my cousins have passed away, moved away etc. but the tie that binds us together were the meals prepared by our beloved Nanny and we will always have these recipes as a guide and reference of how we were loved and comforted by the loving hands that prepared these meals for us and our community hence feed the crowd recipes- gathered with love

A MOTHER'S LOVE

My Parent's separated when I was a little baby and I had the privilege of being raised with my grandparents and cousins in the family home 1219. My mother worked three teaching jobs to pay off college loans and provide for me. My Nanny primarily cooked all of our meals but when my mother and I eventually moved out and I gained a step dad (My Papa Steve) her and I would cook together.

My mom prided herself on making "The perfect rice" as she was taught how to make rice and other delicacies while living in Ghana before I was born. I can remember the aroma of curry as early as six years old because of her curry chicken recipe.

MY mom just like everyone else loved my Nanny's cooking and all you heard was silence during our dinner sessions as everyone's mouths were completely full of enjoyment.

FEED THE CROWD RECIPES
- GATHERED WITH LOVE

Cousin Gwen's Trinidadian rice and stewed chicken pelau

COUSIN GWEN'S TRINIDADIAN RICE AND STEWED CHICKEN PELAU
ONE POT MEAL

Prep time: 10 mins

Cook time: 1 hour

Total time: 1 hr., 10 mins

Serves: 6

Delicious!

Ingredients

- 2 lbs. Chicken
- 2 garlic cloves
- 2 tbsp Ginger
- 1 small onion, chopped
- ½ bunch fresh parsley
- 2 can green pigeon peas
- ½ cup pumpkin
- 2 cups canned coconut milk
- 1 tbsp ketchup
- 1 Maggi cube
- 1 bunches of fresh thyme 1 tbsp coconut oil
- ½ red bell pepper
- 1 tbsp of Worcestershire sauce 3 tbsp white sugar
- ½ cup pimento or 2 habenero peppers chopped
- 1 tsp salt
- 1 tsp Angostura bitters
- 1 stalk of celery chopped
- 4 scallions

- 1 bunch of culantro, chopped
- 2 Tsp of peanut oil
- 1lb of parboiled rice
- 3 tbsp green seasoning
- 2 cups of water

Green seasoning recipe (Make this ahead) – blend 1 stalk of celery, 1 bunch of culantro, 2 cloves of garlic, 1 small onion, ½ bunch of parsley, ½ red bell pepper, 4 scallions, 1 bunch of thyme, 2 pimento peppers or 1 habanero pepper, salt to taste

Caramelized sugar recipe- Coat the bottom of a large stock pot with coconut oil. When oil is hot sprinkle 3 tbsp of white sugar. Stir mixture until it becomes frothy and dark.

1. Clean chicken pieces with fresh lime and season with ginger, parsley, salt and 3 tbsp of green seasoning set aside.
2. In a large stockpot begin the caramelized sugar recipe process. When the sugar becomes dark add seasoned chicken and stir to coat all of the chicken until brown.
3. Cook for 2 to 5 minutes. Add uncooked rice and peas and stir. Add pumpkin, coconut milk, water, 1 habanero pepper and sprinkle the Maggi cube in the pot.
4. Stir continuously and put a lid on the pot in between time. Cook until liquid has completely evaporated and rice is al dente. Remove habanero pepper and serve hot with a side of fresh cucumbers and tomatoes. Enjoy!

Nanny's meatloaf and tomato gravy and potatoes, One pan meal

NANNY'S MEATLOAF WITH TOMATO GRAVY AND POTATOES
ONE PAN MEAL

Prep time: 20 mins

Cook time: 1.5 hours

Total time: 2 hours

Serves: 6-8

Delicious!

Ingredients

- 1.5 pounds russet potatoes, scrubbed and cut into halves
- 2.5 pounds lean ground beef or ground turkey
- 1 large onion, and green bell pepper finely chopped
- 1/4 cup of milk
- 3/4 cup crushed baked buttered biscuits
- 2 eggs
- 2 teaspoons salt
- 1 teaspoon yellow mustard
- 1 teaspoon pepper
- 1/4 teaspoon garlic powder, onion powder and dried parsley

For the glaze:

- 3/4 cup tomato paste
- ½ cup of water
- 1/3 cup light brown sugar
- 2 teaspoons Worcestershire sauce

Directions

1. Single layer cut potatoes on bottom of 6-quart roasting pan around the "wall" of the roasting pan.
2. Soak Mix all other ingredients for loaf in a large bowl. Then form into a loaf before setting it in the middle of roasting pan. Drizzle with olive oil, add 2 cups of water and cover tightly with aluminum foil. Bake on 400 degrees F and check for doneness until internal temperature reaches 155° degrees or higher.
3. In a small bowl, mix ingredients for glaze, then brush on top of loaf.
4. Cover and cook on lowered heat at 375° degrees F for 10 minutes.
5. Serve with potatoes. Enjoy!

FAITH'S ON A BUDGET TUNA NOODLE CASSEROLE

Prep time: 10 mins

Cook time: 10 mins

Total time: 20 mins

Serves: 6

Delicious!

Ingredients

- 15 oz Tuna
- 12 oz Egg noodles
- 15 oz sweet peas, frozen
- 1 can of cream of chicken soup
- 1 tsp black pepper
- 1 tsp salt
- 2 tsp of hot sauce (optional)
- 1 tsp yellow mustard
- 12 cups of mild shredded cheddar cheese
- 1/4 teaspoon garlic powder, onion powder and dried parsley
- Pam spray, olive or vegetable oil (for greasing your baking dish)

Directions

1. Boil Egg Noodles until firm but do not overcook. Drain canned tuna and set aside.
2. Mix all ingredients in a large bowl Except for cheese!
3. Coat baking dish with oil to prevent ticking and place mixture in the dish.

4. Top with shredded cheddar cheese, cover with foil and cook in the oven at 375° degrees F for 10 minutes or until golden brown.
5. Serve hot and Enjoy!

Papa Steve's favorite ham, cheese and potato

casserole Ma' brown recipe

PAPA STEVE'S FAVORITE HAM, CHEESE AND POTATO CASSEROLE MA' BROWN'S RECIPE

Prep time: 15 mins

Cook time: 15 mins

Total time: 30 mins

Serves: 6-8

Delicious!

Ingredients

- 1 stick of butter
- 1 lb. of Russet potatoes, cut into cubes boiled
- 1 can of Condensed Cream of Chicken Soup
- 2 cups of sour cream
- 2 cups of shredded cheddar cheese
- Approx. 2 cups of leftover ham, cut to preferred size.
- Salt and pepper to taste

Directions

1. Preheat oven to 350 degrees.
2. Melt butter in microwave in large bowl.
3. Pour in potatoes, coat well.
4. Mix in condensed soup, sour cream, and cheese.
5. Spread one half of the potato mixture on bottom of 13 x 9 casserole dish.
6. Top the layer with ham.
7. Spread remaining potato mixture over the ham. And cover with remaining shredded cheese.
8. Bake uncovered for 50-60 minutes or until bubbly and golden.
9. Let the casserole sit for 5 minutes before serving. Enjoy!

Grandma Minnie's sweet potato pone, My Dad's favorite!

GRANDMA MINNIE'S SWEET POTATO PONE

MY DAD'S FAVORITE!

Prep time: 15 mins

Cook time: 60 mins

Total time: 1 hour and 15 mins

Serves: 6

Delicious and easy!

Ingredients

- 2 eggs, beaten
- 1/2 cup brown sugar
- 1/4 cup molasses
- 1/4 cup butter, melted
- 1/2 teaspoon salt
- 1/2 teaspoon cinnamon
- 1/2 teaspoon freshly grated nutmeg
- 1/2 cup milk
- Zest of 1 lemon
- 1 medium, sweet potato, about 12 ounces, baked and peeled

1. For best results use a mixer and mix beaten eggs, brown sugar, molasses, butter, salt, cinnamon, and nutmeg until smooth; add the milk, lemon zest, and peeled baked sweet potatoes.
2. Butter a 1 1/2-quart casserole dish. Pour the mixture into the dish. Bake in a preheated 350° oven for 60-75 minutes or until set and golden brown. Serve with vanilla ice cream or whipping cream and Enjoy!

NANNY'S FOOL PROOF ROASTED TURKEY

Prep time: 20 mins

Cook time: 3 hours

Total time:3 hours and 30 mins

Rest for 30 minutes

Serves: 6

Moist and Flavorful

Ingredients

- 12 lb. Turkey, Whole
- 1 large Onion, Whole
- 3 stalks of celery, Whole
- ¼ cup of distilled vinegar
- 1 stick of butter, salted
- 3 tsp paprika
- 3 tsp salt
- 2 tsp black pepper
- 2 tsp garlic powder

Directions

1. Remove turkey from refrigerator and let come to room temperature for about an hour. Preheat oven to 400 degrees. After an hour remove turkey from packaging then remove the neck and gizzard bag from the turkey cavity (discard or save for stock). Pat the turkey dry with paper towels on both the inside and outside. Set Aside.

2. Line a Roasting pan with aluminum foil and place turkey breast side down in the pan.

3. Rub turkey with softened butter. Sprinkle turkey with all seasoning.

4. Stuff turkey with raw onion and fresh celery. Pour distilled vinegar evenly over turkey.

5. Cover turkey with foil and make a "tent" at the top of the turkey. Place on the center rack of the oven and cook for 45 minutes.

6. Lower oven temperature to 325 degrees. Remove turkey from pan and flip it using oven mitts*. The breasts should be up now. Rotate the pan and return turkey to the center rack of the oven and cook for 2-3 hours or until internal temperature reaches 155-165 F degrees. Cover the top of the turkey with foil if the top is getting too browned.

7. Once turkey is cooked through, remove from pan and let rest on a large cutting board for 30 minutes before slicing. Reserve pan drippings for gravy.

Javon's soulful cornbread dressing

JAVON'S SOULFUL CORNBREAD DRESSING

Prep time: 45 mins

Cook time: 1 hour

Total time: 1 hour 45 mins

Serves: 6 -10

Savory!

Ingredients

- 14 oz Cream of chicken
- 3 stalks Celery, chopped
- 3 cloves Garlic, minced
- 3 tsp Sage, dried
- 2 tsp Poultry seasoning
- 1 tsp Black pepper
- 2 tsp Onion powder
- 1 Yellow onion, large chopped
- 1 Green bell pepper, chopped
- 2 Tbsp of white sugar, optional
- 3 Eggs, medium, beaten,
- 4 cups Chicken broth, preferably homemade
- Cooked pieces of turkey or chicken (optional)
- 2 tsp Seasoning salt
- 1 1/3 stick of butter, salted
- 1 cooked can of buttered biscuits
- 1 pan of cooked white cornmeal Cornbread

Directions

1. Cook the cornbread a day in advance according to the instructions on the package. In a saucepan, combine soup with 2 cups of chicken broth. Heat, but do not bring to a boil. Add chopped celery, green bell pepper and onion and cook until tender.

2. In a large baking pan, crumble cooled cornbread. Grab cooked biscuits and crumble/tear those as well. Add your seasonings and salt to your family's taste. Mix well. Add your cooked chopped chicken, celery, bell pepper and onion and the soup mixture and well. You should have 2 cups of Chicken broth remaining, use this if there is any needed liquid. You do not want the mixture to be soupy, but you don't want it too thick either. I usually end up adding the remaining 2 cups to mine, but sometimes I don't need to fill 2 cups, so add it slowly and mix stopping to check the consistency as you go. Taste before adding the beaten eggs to make sure the flavor is according to your liking. Add your 3 beaten eggs, mix well.

3. Slice the sticks of butter and stir throughout the mixture.

4. Add some pats of butter on top to aid in browning and give a slight crispy texture on top.

5. Bake at 400 degrees for 40-45 minutes, every oven is different, so yours might need to cook shorter or longer. When the dressing is completely cooked, you should be able to stick a butter knife in the center and it should come out clean! Serve with cranberry sauce and all of the trimmings Enjoy!

Nanny's Jewish inspired Passover beef brisket

NANNY'S JEWISH INSPIRED PASSOVER BEEF BRISKET

Prep time: 1 hour

Cook time: 7 hours

Total time: 8 hours

Serves: 6

Amazing!

Ingredients

- 7–8 pounds of brisket
- 1 bottle of ketchup
- 1 1/2 cups of Budweiser
- 1 1/2 cups water
- 1.5 tbsp chicken base
- 1/4 cup dehydrated onion flakes
- 6 cloves of garlic (roughly chopped)
- 2 onions (roughly chopped)
- 1 can of crushed tomatoes
- ¼ cup of dark brown sugar
- Salt and pepper to taste

Directions

1. Combine ketchup, water, dehydrated onion, garlic, beer and chicken base and mix to combine.
2. Slather this mixture onto the brisket sneaking it into each nook and cranny.
3. Marinate in the refrigerator for 24 hours.

4. Preheat oven to 350-degrees and place remaining ingredients over brisket in a tightly sealed roasting pan into the oven.

5. Cook for 3-4 hours. Typically, the rule of thumb is an hour a pound. But the true test is when it pulls apart with two forks.

6. Place in refrigerator overnight to cool.

7. Remove fat and cut against the grain NOT with the grain.

8. Place sauce over sliced meat and put into 350- degree oven to warm the meat and sauce. Serve with Nanny's homestyle mashed potatoes, spinach and Enjoy!

FRIED PORK CHOP AND SPANISH RICE
ONE SKILLET MEAL

Prep time: 10 mins
Cook time: 30 mins
Total time: 40 mins
Serves: 6

Ingredients

- 6 Bone in or Boneless Pork chops
- 2 cups of flour
- ¼ tsp salt
- 1 tsp paprika
- ¼ tsp onion powder
- ¼ tsp black pepper
- Vegetable oil for shallow for frying
- 1 bell pepper, chopped small
- 2 celery stalks, chopped small
- 1 yellow onion, chopped small
- 4 ounces of tomato paste
- 2 tbsp Vegetable or Canola Oil
- 1 cup dry long-grain white rice
- 2 cups warm water
- 1 tsp chili powder
- 1 tsp cumin
- 2 tsp chicken bouillon
- 1 tsp minced garlic about 2 cloves
- 1 tsp parsley
- 1 tsp onion powder2 bay leaves
- Salt and pepper to taste

Directions

1. Season pork chops with salt, flour, onion powder and black pepper. Coat with all-purpose flour and lightly shallow fry in a skillet for 2 minutes on each side and set aside.
2. In a large pot add vegetable oil and sauté garlic, bell pepper, celery and onion until translucent and soft.
3. Stir in uncooked rice, tomato paste and seasonings.
4. Mix bouillon with water and stir into rice mixture and add bay leaf.
5. Cover with lid and wait until sauce has reduced to an inch above rice. Add pork chops on top of rice and simmer on low heat until pork chops are tender and rice is al dente. Discard bay leaves and Enjoy!

NANNY'S EASY FRIED SHRIMP, ONION RINGS AND POTATO WEDGES

Prep time: 10 mins

Cook time: 15 mins

Total time: 25 mins

Serves: 6

Golden Delicious!

Ingredients

- Batter ingrtedients
- ½ cup of corn starch
- ½ cup of all-purpose flour
- 1 ½ teaspoon baking powder
- 3/4 teaspoon salt
- pinch of white sugar
- ½ cup of milk
- 1/3 cup of cold unflavored sparkling water
- 1 lb. of extra- large peeled and deveined shrimp
- 1 teaspoon of Cajun seasoning
- 1/4 teaspoon garlic powder, onion powder, salt and black pepper
- 2 large sweet onions, ½- inch thick rings
- 4 extra-large russet potatoes, cut into wedges skin on (place in a bowl of water and soak for at least 30 minutes
- Vegetable, peanut or canola oil for deep frying

Directions

1. Heat cooking oil until it reaches 375 degrees F.
2. Mix all batter ingredients together in a bowl and set aside.
3. Drain potato wedges and pat dry.
4. When cooking oil is ready, fry potato wedges until golden brown and set aside to drain.
5. Dip Shrimp in batter one by one and fry for 2 minutes on each side.
6. Dip onion rings in batter and fry until golden brown on each side. Season all with Cajun seasoning, salt and pepper. Enjoy!

Nanny's Yellow cake with chocolate frosting

NANNY'S YELLOW CAKE WITH CHOCOLATE FROSTING

Prep time: 15mins

Cook time: 45 mins

Total time: 1 hour

Serves: 6- 8

Delicious!

Ingredients

- ¾ cup of butter, unsalted at room temperature
- ¼ cup of oil
- 2 cups of granulated sugar
- 3 large eggs, room temperature
- 1 tbsp pure vanilla extract
- ½ tsp of baking powder
- 1 tsp salt
- 2 2/3 cups Cake flour
- 1 cup of buttermilk, room temperature

Chocolate Frosting

- ½ cup of butter, melted
- 2/3 cups of Dutch unsweetened cocoa powder
- 3 cups of powdered sugar
- 1/3 cup of milk
- 1 tsp pure vanilla extract.

Directions

1. Preheat oven to 350 degrees F. Place parchment in the bottom of two 8–9-inch round cake pans.
2. Cut the paper to fit pans and spray with nonstick cooking spray.
3. In a large bowl, cream sugar and butter until smooth. Add oil and mix. Add the eggs and yolks one at a time, beating after each addition. Add vanilla and mix.
4. Stir together baking powder, salt and sifted cake flour in a medium bowl.
5. Alternate adding in some of the cake flour mixture, stirring to combine and then some of the buttermilk, ending with the flour mixture until just combined. Divide the batter evenly in the pans. Bake for 25-35 minutes or until a toothpick inserted into the center of the cake comes out with no batter. Allow cake to cool.
6. Stir together the butter and cocoa powder. Use hand mixer to beat in the powder sugar, milk and vanilla until light and fluffy for several minutes. Once the cake is cool, frost with chocolate frosting and Enjoy!

Judi's Chicken curry

JUDI'S EASY CHICKEN CURRY AND THE PERFECT WHITE RICE

Prep time: 10 mins

Cook time: 30 mins

Total time: 40 mins

Serves: 6

Amazing!

Ingredients

- 1.5 2 tablespoons coconut oil
- 1/2 medium onion, finely minced
- 1 head of garlic, chopped (10–12 cloves)
- 2 tablespoons ginger, minced
- 1 tablespoon each: paprika, ground cumin, coriander, and turmeric
- 1 teaspoon cayenne powder, optional
- 3 chicken breasts or bone- in chicken, chopped into bite-sized pieces
- 1 28-ounce can have condensed cream of chicken
- 2 teaspoons sea salt and black pepper
- 2 celery stalks, chopped
- 2 carrots, chopped
- 1 cup of water

The perfect rice:

- 2 cups Jasmine rice
- 4 cups of water
- 2 tsp oil

Rinse the starch off the Jasmine rice. Bring water and oil to a boil in a small pot. Add rice to boiling water and stir. Once boiling is reached, cover pot with lid and reduce heat. Let simmer until water is fully absorbed. Turn off pot and let rice sit with lid for at least 5 minutes. Use a fork to scrape up rice so the rice will not become mushy- Judi's perfect rice!

Directions

1. Season chicken with paprika, ginger, cumin, coriander, salt and pepper set aside.
2. In a large skillet, add garlic, carrots, celery and carrots to coconut oil.
3. Sauté chicken and cook on all sides for at least 2 minutes until brown.
4. Combine turmeric, cayenne powder and water to condensed cream of chicken.
5. Mix with chicken and vegetable mixture and stir thoroughly. Cover and let simmer until veggies are fork tender and chicken is done. Serve with rice and Enjoy!

ABOUT THE AUTHOR

Javon McCain Nicholas has an insatiable hunger for all thing's food!

She used her former career path to become an entrepreneur and food enthusiast! She looks forward to delighting your tastebuds with her recipes, virtual cooking classes, workshops and product line. Please stay connected to her social media platforms Chow On Eats and So Chef-ish and YouTube channel Chow On Eats! She currently resides in the Midwest with her husband and two cats!